IMAGES
of England

BUXTON

An aerial view of Lower Buxton taken in about 1930. The centre is dominated by the Devonshire Royal Hospital, Palace Hotel and the Georgian Crescent but the view also shows part of Devonshire Park and Cavendish Girls School (top left), Lightwood (top right), and the Town Hall at the edge of the Market Place (bottom right). A later shot, with a similar viewpoint to this, was used in many of the town guides in the1950s and '60s.

IMAGES
of England

BUXTON

Compiled by
Mike Bentley, Mike Langham and Colin Wells

TEMPUS

First published 1999
Copyright © Mike Bentley, Mike Langham and Colin Wells, 1999

Tempus Publishing Limited
The Mill, Brimscombe Port,
Stroud, Gloucestershire, GL5 2QG

ISBN 0 7524 1586 7

Typesetting and origination by
Tempus Publishing Limited
Printed in Great Britain by
Midway Clark Printing, Wiltshire

J.R Board as a young man and J.D. Meddins as a young boy in the processing room of Watsons in Sheffield in about 1912.

Contents

J.R. Board and his wife Elizabeth Meddins in around 1914.

J.D. Meddins in around 1950.

Introduction

A Board's Eye View

Buxton, high in the hills of the Peak District, has attracted visitors throughout time. In Roman times it was a spa of some importance; a place of rest and recuperation for legionnaires returning from the northern borders. It enjoyed great popularity in late Mediaeval times when Mary Queen of Scots visited to take the waters on five occasions between 1573 and 1584 and brought in her trail important members of the Elizabethan court including Robert Dudley, the Earl of Leicester, and Lord Burghley, the Lord Treasurer. Buxton was developed as a Georgian spa by the Fifth Duke of Devonshire who commissioned the architect, John Carr of York, to design a magnificent crescent, new baths and stables between 1780 and 1789. But its heyday was reached in the nineteenth century when Buxton became a health resort to rival Harrogate and Bath. The last century saw phenomenal growth of population, accommodation and medicinal facilities in the town and many people came to take the waters and receive water-based and associated treatments for their ailments. This reputation continued into the early part of the twentieth century, though the development of the town was, inevitably, shaped by two World Wars and, as interest in water medicine declined, Buxton had to build a reputation as an inland resort and conference centre.

This book is about post First World War Buxton. It looks at the life of the town through the lenses of a small firm of commercial photographers who gained a solid and reliable reputation for their work. It offers a unique insight into twentieth-century Buxton. The development of photography in the middle of the nineteenth century provided the means of recording a visual history of the town as it grew during that time. There were commercial photographers in Buxton from the early days of photography, beginning with the pioneer Barrowclough Wright Bentley in 1851. As the technology rapidly developed others set up in business including B.W. Bentley's cousin, William Bentley, and his successor John Hobbis. By the end of the century yet others such as, D.C. Latham of Station Road, Professor Simpson and Arundel Hall in Spring Gardens and W.G. Hosler in the Quadrant were making a living in the town. In 1911 Robert F. Hunter established a photographic shop and studio at Grafton House, no.1 the Quadrant. R.F. Hunter quickly forged a reputation opening a 'new American electric studio' under the direction of Mr E.C. Iliffe late of W.W. Winter photography, Derby. Soon after the firm was established Hunter also took on a young photographer by the name of James Robert Board. By 1916 the business had moved to no. 9 Cavendish Circus with darkroom premises in the Old Court House, George Street. J.R. Board originated from Sheffield where he had worked and probably trained with a photographic firm called Watsons. He moved to Buxton in the early part of the twentieth century continuing his photographic career with Hunters and, when R.F. Hunter left to further his fortunes in London, Board took over the business From 1926 Board's Buxton business was very successful and he quickly gained a reputation for quality which attracted such worthies to his studio as David Lloyd George, George Bernard Shaw and the family of the Dukes of Devonshire, to be the subjects of his portraiture. As a commercial photographer Board covered a large range of subjects from townscapes to portraiture, events, publicity, advertising, postcards and general scenes of life in Buxton. J.R. Board, when not behind the camera lens or in the darkroom, had interests which included zoology and history. He was born in 1888 and served for four years with the Royal Engineers in the First World War and during this time was quite severely gassed, an experience which was thought to have contributed to his relatively early death at the age of 54. He was a conservative by political persuasion and was a member of the Constitutional Club. His wife, Elizabeth was sixteen years older than he and they did not have any children. She had a son, John, by a previous marriage who was adopted as Board's stepson upon their marriage. She had her own drapery shop at 49 High Street, Buxton and despite her marriage to Board, traded under her first married name of Meddins. John also became involved in photography from an early age. Born in Buxton in 1900 he was brought up in Byron Street and educated at Kent's Bank school. At fifteen he went to work as a photographer's assistant for W.G. Hosler gaining experience in darkroom work, printing, developing and enlarging, for three years before enlisting in the army. He joined his step-father during the time of Hunter's business in Buxton and they worked together until Board died in 1943. John Davis Meddins took over the firm from that time but still continued to trade under the name of 'Board's of Buxton', a name which had by then become synonymous with quality. The retirement of Meddins in about 1968 brought about another change of ownership and the business was taken over by Roy Turner who continued under the same trading name until his retirement in about 1980. On Turner's retirement the business was wound up. Over more than forty years, Board and his stepson, John Meddins produced a large collection of photographs using old-style half-plate cameras. Many of these photographs are now stored, together with their glass negatives, at the Buxton Museum and Art Gallery. Two of the authors of this book have spent much time cataloguing this unique collection and the quality and diversity of the Board photographs became the driving force to put this pictorial history together. This book is comprised of a wide cross section of the collection which spans the years 1925-1968. Virtually all were taken by either J.R. Board or J.D. Meddins.

This collection of photographs represents the first twentieth-century pictorial history of the town. Many residents and visitors will remember 'Buxton - the Spa of Blue Waters' as it is portrayed in these pictures, others will see these views of the town for the very first time. Through the eye of Board's camera it is possible for all to see the changes which have taken place. We hope the experience will be both enjoyable and a fitting legacy to twentieth-century Buxton as we prepare to enter the twenty first century and a new millennium.

An advertisement from the Buxton Town Guide of 1927.

8

One
The Changing Face
of Commerce

W.R. Sanders (1920) Ltd were situated at the southern end of Spring Gardens, adjacent to the Picture House. In 1921 they advertised as main distributing agents in North Derbyshire for: Austin, Armstrong Siddeley, Standard, Rover, Belsize, and Overland cars, also Sunbeam Motor Cycles.

By 1932, when these two photographs were taken, Sanders were specialising in Austin, Humber, Morris and Riley cars. In the showroom is a Singer Eight and an Austin Ten.

The Sanders' workshop extended up Holker Road. The houses shown were still quite new when photographed here in 1932. Later, Sanders garage was acquired by the Kenning Motor Group.

The motor business of G. Oram in the Old Court House, George Street in the mid 1960s. By this time the firm also had an agency for Renault cars. The building was known as the New Court House in 1870 and provided the magistrate's court. It was also the office of the the Buxton Local Board (the early form of the local authority) and the Devonshire Buxton Estate office.

G. Oram bought his property in the Old Courthouse from the Duke of Devonshire in late 1955 and opened his showrooms there in 1956. This photograph, taken at about that time, shows two new cars for sale, a Standard Eight and an Austin A30.

Miller's popular cafe at 19 Spring Gardens has changed its appearance several times over the years. Here it is in February 1938.

The interior of Miller's Cafe in 1933.

By April 1938 the cafe had been given a face-lift and offered 'Miller's Modern Bar' on the ground floor.

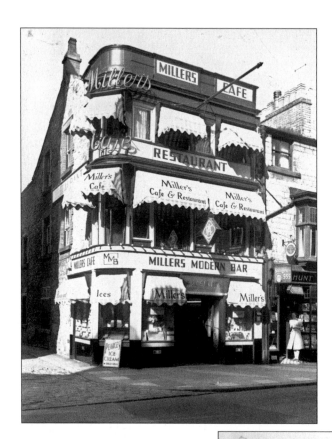

The later addition of blinds and lights enhances the attractiveness of the frontage.

By the 1960s the frontage was further changed losing its elegant curved windows to the first floor. Note that by this time Millers had taken in Hunts the tobacconist from next door. Today Millers cafe is a little further down Spring Gardens.

This view of Terry's Corner House Cafe was taken in September 1938. The Quadrant at this time still has some colonnading.

The rather elegant interior of this cafe in 1937 with tables set for afternoon tea.

J.R. Board was badly gassed in the First World War and the lack of wartime photographs amongst his collection could be ascribed to his reluctance to cover the Second World War. It is more likely, however, that restrictions were placed on what could be photographed. This scene is of the sandbagging of the Post Office in the Quadrant, opposite Board's own shop.

Part of the war effort was to collect aluminium to make aeroplanes and the people of Buxton worked very hard for this purpose. Here the Women's Voluntary Service are running a collecting shop in Spring Gardens.

'Potatoes are fuel for the body' says one of the signs extolling the value of this staple diet in wartime. The shop is Rosemans on Spring Gardens.

The library of The Boots Company in Spring Gardens looks a calm haven in August 1938, one year before the beginning of the Second World War.

The premises of J.R. Board were at the top of Cavendish Circus opposite Devonshire Road. In the 1930s more than one lorry ran out of control down the long, fairly steep gradient, with disastrous consequences. In February 1934 one such lorry ended up in Board's shop. These two scenes give a whole new meaning to the slogan, 'Photographs developed while you wait'!

The Lancashire and Yorkshire Bank was at 20 Spring Gardens and by 1929, when this picture was taken, had just become Martin's Bank.

The interior of the bank in 1929. It is reminiscent of Captain Mainwairing's bank in *Dad's Army*.

The earliest bank in Higher Buxton was a sub-branch of the Sheffield and Rotherham Bank (later Williams Deacon's) opened in 1899 at number 43 High Street. This branch of the Westminster Bank is at No.45 on the opposite side of Ash Street. The photograph was taken in April 1934.

In Higher Buxton this long-established ironmongers, owned by Shaw Brothers, was at 9 and 11 Market Street. They were advertised as 'The Household Stores' and this view of 1931 shows an extensive display of wares available.

If you visited P. Bennett and Son, Funeral Furnisher's premises in Torr Street in 1932, you might have been shown into this rather quaint looking parlour.

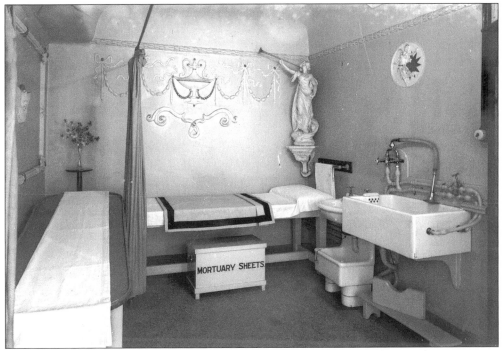

The mortuary of P. Bennett and Son was in Torr Street. This photograph was taken in January 1932.

Ball & Co. House Furnishers had extensive showrooms in the Market Place which are seen here in June 1931.

Furniture from Ball's would be delivered in this Model T Ford van photographed here outside the Palace Hotel in November 1928.

Buxton has been an inland resort since the time of the Romans and provides an extensive range of accommodation. The oldest building in town, the Old Hall, was built as a Derbyshire square house by the Sixth Earl of Shrewsbury in 1572/3 to provide accommodation for Mary Queen of Scots. The captive queen came to Buxton on five occasions between 1573 and 1584, usually for several weeks in the Summer, to take the waters for her various illnesses. The Old Hall has operated continuously as a hotel from that time. This photograph of the hotel with blinds was used extensively in advertising during the early 1960s.

This hotel appears regularly in Buxton town guides throughout the 1920s and 30s and the photograph dates from about 1935. The property, built in 1876, is situated on St John's Road adjacent to St John's churchyard.

The Empire Hotel was built by Spiers & Pond, the high-class railway buffet catering firm, and opened in 1903. It had a magnificent situation in Buxton Park as will be seen from this view which dates from the early part of this century. It had a short commercial life becoming a discharge centre for Canadian troops in the First World War after which it never reopened as a hotel.

Buxton, in the early part of the Second World War, became almost like a garrison town with many hotels, including the Empire, occupied by troops. After the war squatters moved in and this photograph shows the hotel during their occupation.

In 1949 the squatters were removed but this was not before they had faced the harsh winter of 1947, as this photograph shows. The Empire Hotel was demolished in 1964.

Views like this one of the Argyle Hotel at the Burlington Road end of Broad Walk appeared frequently in their advertisements, though this particular shot may not have been used since none of them featured the Austin A30 car outside. J.R. Board placed his own car in some photographs, if his successor John Meddins did the same we may be looking at his car here!

The Buckingham Hotel on Burlington Road in the 1930s. The hotel was formerly two houses known as Rockavon and Buckingham, built 1875/6. In the latter part of the nineteenth century the artist George S. Ramsay lived at Buckingham House where he painted dainty and colourful views of the area, many of which were used as postcards. He is commemorated by the present-day 'Ramsay's Bar'.

Across the road from the Buckingham is the Portland Hotel which stands on St John's Road and was built in the early 1870s as Portland Villas. The unusual sight of an RAC patrol man on point duty dates this photograph probably to the 1940s.

This picture of the Roseleigh Hotel on Broad Walk was taken for the Buxton Guide of 1960. The hotel was 'under the personal supervision of the proprietress (Mrs) B.J. Adams' and it advertised an '...unrivalled position - overlooking the Pavilion Gardens...', with '...hot and cold water and gas fires in bedrooms...'.

The Railway Hotel on Bridge Street was built in 1864 by the Chesterfield Brewery Company. It is remarkable how unchanged the 'Railway' has remained. Its appearance in this photograph of about 1950 is very similar to that in an engraving of the hotel produced nearly 100 years before.

The Cheshire Cheese on High Street is a late eighteenth-century carrier's inn. The rear of the inn, as shown, was cobbled and would have had provision for stabling and storage. This photograph could be described as timeless, certainly the back of the 'Cheese' would have looked like this up to the middle of this century.

The well-known wine and spirit firm of J.L. Denman & Co. Ltd., had premises at 8 Spring Gardens, shown here in 1935.

Denman's also kept a store in Victoria (now Holker) Avenue, behind the White Lion public house.

Denman's delivery van outside the Palace Hotel photographed in 1930.

The Maypole grocery shop presents an eyecatching display on Spring Gardens in 1929.

This modernized version of the Maypole shop from the 1960s certainly lacks some of the style of the earlier one.

This interior of the shop seen in the early 1960s shows well stacked shelves and a staff eager to serve! In the centre is the manager, Trevor Hobday.

The corner of Spring Gardens and Hardwick Street in 1928. On the left is a glimpse of the colonnading of E.C. Milligan's drapery shop. Premises on the right include the Lancashire & Yorkshire Bank, 20 Spring Gardens and the International grocery stores next door.

This later view dating from the early 1950s shows Denman's the wine and spirit merchants and Collinson's cafe on the left of the picture. The delivery boy on his specially designed bike would be a rare sight today.

The Hardwick Hotel and off-licence sales on Spring Gardens.

The Home and Colonial Stores in Spring Gardens photographed in May 1929.

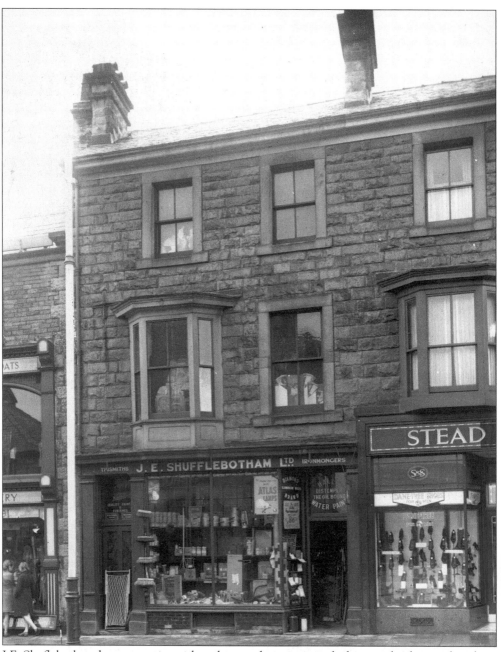

J.E. Shuflebotham began as a tinsmith making and repairing such things as buckets and cooking utensils by hand but by the time of this photograph in 1946 the business was mainly ironmongery. The photograph of the shop on Spring Gardens was taken for Curry's prior to them acquiring the premises and carrying out a complete refit.

This view of the Crescent in the late 1920s shows the bathchair stand to the left with Turner's Memorial, acting as a roundabout, to the right.

The Whaley Bridge and Buxton Cooperative Society Emporium at the southern end of Spring Gardens shown on 8 December 1934, the year of its opening. With the Spa Cinema across the road this introduced a distinct Art Deco influence at this end of the street (see p. 57).

W.H. Smith's are remembered particularly for their station book stalls. This one was on the Midland station at Buxton. The London & North Western station had a branch of Wymans.

These shops on Fairfield Road have long since closed. The photograph, taken just after The Second War shows the shops of the London Central Meat Company and J.B Walker, hay, corn, seed and hardware store. London Central Meat also had a shop in High Street.

How many people remember open-fronted fish and game shops, like this one, inviting customers in to select their purchases? Cod fillets at 8d (about 3p) in 1937 look cheap today. Spring flowers are also on offer.

In addition to the branch in Spring Gardens the International Stores had a shop in Higher Buxton. The alleyway to the right is known as 'Wood's Gennel' after the grocery shop of Woods which previously stood on the same site. The date of the photograph is about 1938.

The Opera House, financed by the Buxton Gardens Company and built by the prolific theatre architect, Frank Matcham in 1903. The theatre, together with the whole of the Pavilion Gardens complex, was acquired in 1927 by the local authority from its previous owners, the Buxton Gardens Company. Shown here in 1938 when it was operating mainly as a cinema, the theatre is, however, advertising the approaching visit of the Old Vic Company for the Buxton Theatre Festival.

Two
Inland Resort

The Opera House interior during its long period of use as a cinema and before the 1979 restoration. This view shows the ornate proscenium arch and the elaborate boxes. Frank Matcham was a pioneer in the use of cantilevering to support the upper storeys of the auditorium in order to maximise the audience viewing area and reduce the number of columns to support them. This is a good example of his technique.

A view of the projection room at the Opera House, 1932. A projection room survives today at the rear of the Gallery and is conveniently placed to house 'follow-spot' lanterns. Few productions at the theatre nowadays require to use follow-spots and very often their annual outing is during the Christmas pantomime.

A view of the Opera House taken from the upper floors of the George Hotel. From 1932 the theatre was used almost exclusively as a cinema. The building fell into disrepair during this period and in 1978 the cinema company was persuaded to give up the remaining years of its lease of the building, making way for the subsequent 1979 restoration and re-opening as a theatre. The re-opening also incorporated the inauguration of the International Opera Festival which is now in its twenty first year.

The approach to the Opera House and the entrance to the Pavilion Gardens seen here in about 1929.

An unusual view of part of the iron and glass pavilion taken during the annual illuminations in the Pavilion Gardens in the 1960s.

It became something of a tradition for many people during the late 1950s and 1960s to visit the 'Buxton's Illuminations' in the Pavilion Gardens. Trees, buildings and specially constructed displays were lit in much the same way as they are today at Matlock Bath.

The interior of the Concert Hall at the Pavilion Gardens in about 1930 showing the original dome windows which nowadays cannot be seen from the inside because of the introduction of a false ceiling to the hall. The organ at the rear of the hall was originally positioned in the Pavilion Central Hall and was moved when the Concert Hall was added to the complex in 1876.

The Pavilion Gardens complex has hosted a wide range of entertainments since it was first opened, and it still does. The following series illustrates some of the variety. Here we see boxing bouts in 1960.

Canines on the catwalk in a dog show at the Concert Hall, c. 1960.

The latest fashions on show in the late 1950s.

Another busy day at the Pavilion Gardens. Coaches parked on the Promenade in the late 1950s.

A delightful venue for ballroom dancing in about 1959. Judging from the numbers on the backs of the men and the judge to the left, this was a competitive event.

A stand in the Retail Fruit Federation's exhibition at Buxton, c. 1959.

Children enjoying entertainment from Harry Corbett and his glove puppet, Sooty, in the 1960s.

The impressive looking Gold Coast Police Band on stage in 1947.

This display at a horticultural show in about 1960 also shows off the Large Concert Hall or 'Octagon' to good effect.

The Pavilion Gardens has, today, a well equipped children's playground but in 1959, as seen here, there was also plenty to keep the children amused.

A favourite picnic area by the river Wye which winds its way through the Pavilion Gardens.

The same river provides paddling facilities in 1937.

This view from about 1946 was probably taken from the Buckingham Hotel on Burlington Road and shows the tennis courts which occupied the ground now used as a car park.

Pavilion Gardens bowling green at the south east corner of the grounds recorded during tennis week in 1927. In its heyday this was acknowledged to be one of the finest crown greens in the North of England.

Boating on the upper lake at the Pavilion Gardens, *c.* 1930. During the winter months the level of this lake was lowered and skating was allowed on the frozen surface. During the refurbishments taking place at the time of writing it is intended that boating be reintroduced on the large lake.

The Pavilion Gardens had a permanent model railway exhibition in the 1960s on the ground which is nowadays occupied by the car park. This shows the extensive layout.

Another view of the 'Daveland' model railway exhibition in the 1960s showing the operator, Mr Bacon, who was a railway booking clerk.

The terraced walks or the Slopes, c. 1930. When first designed the area was known as St Anne's Cliff. After a re-landscaping in 1818 by Sir Jeffrey Wyatville the name changed to the Terraces and later became known as the Slopes. The foreground shows the St Anne's Well building (formerly the pump room) shortly before the removal of the pepper pot domes on either side.

Morris dancing at the base of the Slopes in the 1950s. This view shows a little of the interior of the glass and iron canopy outside the Hot Baths building.

A view of the war memorial on the Slopes taken between the two world wars before the area around its base was paved and walled. Another memorial in the form of a plaque can be seen at the bottom of Bennett Street which lists the fallen from the First World War.

The dressing of wells with flowers, seeds and other natural products to form a scene, often biblical, is a widespread custom in Derbyshire towns and villages. It is thought to be a pagan form of thanksgiving to the Gods for the water supply, though the custom was later adopted as a Christian festival. The custom was revived in Buxton in 1840 and has developed into a popular festival held in July which includes the blessing of the wells, crowning of the festival queen, displays of dancing, decorated streets and shops, a pageant and procession and visit by the fun-fair. The following sequence gives a flavour of this 'people's festival'. Here is St Anne's Well in The Crescent at the 1952 well dressing. The Duke of Devonshire was the mayor of Buxton for that year and he is here accompanied by the Duchess and their two children (in sailor suits). The Festival queen was Brenda Gilman.

The queen for 1956, Doreen Wardle, is seen here with her entourage on the float in The Crescent.

In 1949 the Princess Elizabeth and the Duke of Edinburgh visited Buxton at well dressing time. The Festival Queen, fifteen year old Joan Mellor, who was presented to the future Queen of England, said, 'It was the most exciting moment of my life'.

A rather unusual form of transport for Queen Eileen Edge in 1927.

It was usual for everyone in the street where the well dressing queen lived to decorate their houses. This photograph shows the whole of Hollins Street and Hollins Avenue transformed into 'Clematis Drive' in 1952.

The carnival procession, until a few years ago, began on Fairfield Common and travelled down Fairfield Road into the town. Here the queen's float makes its way down past the junction of Queen's Road in the 1950s.

The scouts here have won first prize for their entry in the carnival. The picture shows a young Bill Weston and Mick Radcliffe standing (behind the front wing of this Austin Seven) on North road, Fairfield. Their theme of 'Ten Year Test' dates this picture to 1960, the year that the MOT was introduced for motor vehicles of ten years and over.

Dancing troupes or 'majorettes' are a particular feature of the well dressing festival. The Fairfield Majorettes are seen here on North Road, Fairfield, prior to the commencement of the carnival procession, having won first prize. The mascot lead is Jean Lomas followed by Pat Millett, Stephanie Baker, Beatrice Oldham, -?-, Jean Lee, Wendy Bates, Diane Redfern, Sheila Barber and Lindsey Richards. Note also, behind the display of young ladies, the long demolished cottages which bordered St Peter's churchyard. The photograph dates from about 1957.

The Picture House stood at the corner of Holker Road and Spring Gardens. It is seen here in about 1925.

The Art Deco style Spa Cinema, built in 1937, replaced the Picture House which had stood on the same site. Architects were Naylor & Sale of Derby and Nottingham. For many years the Spa and the Opera house competed for the town's cinema business. This view dates from 1946. During the 1970s the Spa was used as a bingo hall and later reverted to use as a cinema again with two smaller auditoriums to maximise income, but this did not arrest the decline of interest and the building was demolished in 1986.

The Playhouse 1938. Built in 1889 by local architect W. R. Bryden and financed by the Buxton Improvements Company. The chairman of the company, Dr Robertson, was of the opinion that theatre was a rather vulgar thing and would not allow the building to be so called. In deference to his wishes the building was originally named 'The Entertainment Stage'. it was soon renamed the 'New Theatre' or the 'Pavilion Theatre'. In 1903 it was renamed 'The Hippodrome' and was used as a cinema until 1932. In 1935 it was again in use as a theatre and was renamed the 'Playhouse'.

The Hippodrome on St Johns Road, 1931. An interior view showing the elaborate Moorish murals which were painted. From 1945 The Buxton Repertory Company performed regularly at the Playhouse and household names like Nigel Hawthorne, Patrick Cargill and Joan Sanderson were regular cast members. More latterly the Playhouse was kept alive by local devotees such as the Buxton Theatre and Arts Trust and the local amateur drama and operatic groups. With the refurbishment of the Opera House in 1979 it was converted into a multi-purpose exhibition and meeting hall and was once again renamed, this time the Paxton Suite.

The Ashwood Park on the South Eastern entrance to the town, another busy recreation area, shown here in the 1930s. The photograph was probably taken to be used on a postcard.

This view of Ashwood Park looking north provides a good panorama of the eastern side of the town. The bowling green is still used today but the bowlers' hut is not as stylish as this one. The river Wye on the left makes its way out of town through this park. This photograph was used in the 1939 Buxton Guide.

Steeple jacks work on the spire of the Wesleyan Methodist church in Devonshire Park. When this photograph was taken, in 1928, it had become the Christian Science Church in Buxton. Houses now occupy the site in Devonshire Road.

Three
Spiritual Buxton

This Buxton church, St Mary's in Dale Road, is a real gem and has probably been underrated architecturally. It was designed by P. Currey and C. C. Thompson in the Arts and Crafts style in 1914-15. Inside, the fittings are contemporary as can be seen from this image taken in about 1930. The work is close to that of the Northern Art Workers Guild of the early 1900s.

Major work was carried out to the roof of St John's church in 1937. Extensive dry rot was found in the timbers and immediate replacement was needed. As will be seen from these photographs, the old roof was completely removed and steel girders were used to support the new roof.

A crane with a substantial gib was required to reach and handle the new steelwork for St John's church roof. Here is another view of the repairs in progress, taken in August 1937.

The photographer as artist – St John's churchyard in winter.

St Anne's church contains many interesting objects. The altar rail and gate were made by Mr Benjamin Simpson, the founder of Ben Simpson's Boys Club in the town. He was a devoted worshipper and served for forty nine years as choirmaster and sacristan. The roof of the sanctuary is painted with scenes depicting the 'Te Deum' or the servants of God united in his praise.

Substantial repairs to the roof of St Anne's church, Bath road took place in 1956-7. An interesting view of houses on Spencer Road is revealed.

The Salvation Army Hall is seen here, on the right of this row of buildings, in the1940s. The complex of buildings occupied the former stables to the Eagle Hotel on the Market Place. In the middle is the Spa Garage of F.H. Andrews & Co. and on the left the lounge bar of the Spa Hotel, known as the Spa Bar.

St James church on Bath Road was built in 1870/71 to cater for the substantial increase in population and visitors to the Victorian health resort. The spire was removed in about 1896 for safety reasons and the church demolished in the 1950s. This photograph, taken in February 1931, shows the great size of this church, designed by M.H. Taylor in the perpendicular style. It could seat 750 people.

This late 1920s view, taken from the roof of the Crescent, shows on the right the spire of the Congregational church and, behind it, the tower of Trinity church.

The Roman Catholic church of St Anne, on Terrace Road, was built by Robert Rippon Duke in 1861 and designed by J.J. Scoles in the lancet style. Earlier Scoles had supervised the building of the striking Classical style church of All Saints (RC) at Hassop. This view of St Anne's taken in 1950 shows the nave and chancel and, to the left, the Lady Chapel.

Interior of St Peter's church Fairfield taken in March 1936 and showing the degree to which worship was centred in the chancel at that time with the choir and clergy separated from the congregation. Today it is much more inclusive and this is reflected in the repositioning of the choir stalls and the pulpit in the crossing aisles. The large wooden tablets either side of the altar contain the ten commandments and are now situated in the south crossing aisle.

The North Western Co. motor bus makes its way slowly up Terrace Road in this delightful early
1930s view. The bus, registered DB9358, was supplied new in 1930. It is built on a Tillings
Stevens chassis with a body by Brush of Loughborough. The bus was rebodied in 1935 by the
Eastern Counties Carriage Co. and returned to North Western. It was withdrawn from service
in 1941.

Four

Out and About

A floodlit Crescent and Hot Baths. At this time, in 1959, the old Crescent Hotel (centre) was being used as an annex to the Devonshire Hospital.

Entering Buxton from the south the A6 passes Ashwood Park, part of which is shown here on the right. At the time of this picture, in the late 1920s, the A6 continued up through the centre of town and over Long Hill. The road in the centre was the A624 leading to Fairfield and beyond. Outside the Ashwood Park Hotel stands a charabanc. Notice also the fields at the back right showing that much of the Fairfield 'new estate' had yet to be built.

Just beyond the Fairfield Road junction the road enters Buxton under the great viaduct built by the LNW Railway company in 1891/2. It is over 900 feet in length and rises to a height of about 90 feet carrying the line from Buxton to Ashbourne. This view, taken in the late 1920s, looks peaceful enough though just under the viaduct Spring Gardens, one of the principal commercial streets would, one imagines, have presented a busier picture.

Another southern entrance into the town at Sherbrook on the A515 Ashbourne Road. The house in the centre is Sherbrook Lodge still with its beautifully landscaped gardens, seen here in 1938. It is now a youth hostel. The road going up on the right leads to Harpur Hill.

This photograph, taken in 1938, shows an eight wheeler ERF lorry loaded with hydrated lime from Hindlow Quarry. A number of quarries border the south west of the town and limestone processing has always been an important industry. The lorry is standing on the Dukes Drive, a scenic carriageway built in 1796, which connects the two southern entrances to the town. The viaduct in the background carries the LNW Railway between Buxton and Ashbourne.

The Old Hall Hotel, Devonshire Hospital and Pavilion Gardens as seen from the Town Hall. The massive Empire Hotel can be seen on the left at the rear. In the left foreground are the Georgian town houses of Hall Bank.

A panorama showing Lower Buxton from the Town Hall. On the left of this view is the Midland Railway station which was designed and built to match its neighbouring station, the LNW Railway. The LNW Railway line can be seen sweeping over Spring Gardens on its way south. The picture was taken prior to November 1935 when the Midland Railway depot closed.

The photographer was here standing on Palace Fields, now occupied by the schools of St Thomas More and St Anne. The Edwardian houses, built by Farrow & Brindley, on Lightwood Road can be seen on the left. Lansdowne Road in 1927, the year of this photograph, was undeveloped at its eastern end (centre of photograph) and the bridge at the bottom of Brown Edge Road had newly replaced the ford.

Undeveloped fields south of the junction of Green Lane and College Road. The houses on Green lane are comparatively new. In the wider view of the town can be seen such landmarks as the Devonshire Hospital dome, the Empire and Palace Hotels. The field on the right used to be a popular toboggan run in the winter.

In 1956 a new caravan site was licensed to operate in the disused Corbar quarry on Manchester Road. This shows the procession leaving the Crescent for the opening ceremony.

Visitors inspect the new caravan site facilities in 1956. In the 1960 Buxton Guide the Punch Bowl Caravan and Camping Site declared itself to be the most up-to-date caravan park in Britain and offered, three ablutions with WCs, hot and cold wash basins, baths, showers, laundry with Bendix washer and a licensed club.

Looking south from Corbar. The dome of the Devonshire Hospital, the Crescent and the Town Hall can all be seen in this view.

A fine panorama of the town looking eastwards from Corbar Hill. Note that the bottom of Lansdowne Road is now built upon which suggests that the date is probably the mid-1930s.

Greetings from
BUXTON

Postcards were an important aspect of the photographer's business in a holiday town such as Buxton. This is a favourite view of the town taken from the Town Hall in about 1930. It shows the Georgian Crescent designed by John Carr of York and built 1780-84. It will be observed that The Slopes in the foreground are planted with quite young trees. This magnificent view of the town shows the Palace Hotel in the centre background and to its left the Devonshire Royal Hospital with its impressive dome of 138 feet inner diameter.

MARKET PLACE

Greetings from
BUXTON

THE CRESCENT

TOWN CENTRE

ASHWOOD PARK

Multi-view postcards are still popular. This one, produced in the 1950s, uses photographs taken over a number of years. The aerial centre picture is of particular interest, it shows a rather stylised rock formation in the right foreground which didn't exist in reality. This photograph was used on a number of brochures in the mid-1930s advertising the town and its conference facilities.

Postcard view of the Hot Baths in about 1960. The chicken wire around the new plantings on the slopes is not particularly photogenic but this is a good view of the Hot Baths before the colonnading was removed in the 1970s.

The delights of the Pavilion Gardens are shown here in five views published as a postcard in the 1960s.

An art class at Buxton College in the 'Widdows' block. This quadrangle of pavilion-style classrooms were added to the Buxton College in 1928/9 by George Widdows, architect to the Derbyshire County Council. They have been retained in the new Buxton Community School opened in 1993.

The 'Maison Rouge' or Red House was designed by the Leek architect, Larner Sugden, in 1897 in the Arts and Crafts style. It stood in the Buxton Park Ring. At the time of this photograph, in the 1960s, it had become an annex to the Normanton private school. Sadly it later fell into disrepair and was demolished.

Unfortunately J.R. Board took very few photographs around the Harpur Hill and Burbage areas of the town. Luckily in 1928 he did take, for whatever reason, four interesting shots off the Leek Road, two of which are shown here. This picture shows the deserted main road towards Ladmanlow. The corner, near the present Rock Bay service station was straightened out in the 1960s.

This view looks across towards Edgemoor and shows a very sparsely housed Macclesfield Old Road.

The Town Hall lit to good advantage, here in around 1960. It is now lit again in the evenings in much the same way.

A floodlit view of St Johns church in 1960.

The George Hotel was built in the late eighteenth century to front onto the original Manchester Road. In the nineteenth century it was an important part of the estate of hotels owned by the Duke of Devonshire providing accommodation for the spa visitor.

Part of the George Hotel, now George Mansions, from Manchester Road.

Marlborough Mansions on Marlborough Road are a good example of the numerous nineteenth-century apartment blocks to be found in Buxton. These were designed by the local architect, William Radford Bryden. At the time of this photograph (about 1926) self-contained, unfurnished flats were on offer. Notice the boy and his bike in the entrance standing in front of the Bullnosed Morris car.

Here Boards or Meddins took what appears to be a speculative shot from the rear of the Crescent. It was taken before 1967 and shows the roofs of the Charity Hot Baths and drinking well in George Street in the foreground. The Devonshire Royal Hospital is separated from the Palace Hotel on the right by Devonshire Road.

The Barms, or Fairfield Common, in about 1938 with St Peters Road and Fairfield church on the left. Nunsfield Farm is in the centre.

A solitary car motors on the A624 (now A6) across Fairfield Common in about 1938.

St Anne's Well, *c.* 1920. Originally built as the Pump Room in 1894 the building was enlarged by filling in the open arcading on the front of the building in 1912. After this enlargement the water was served from the marble well at the rear of the building and not as before from pumps at the serving counter. For this reason it was renamed St Anne's Well.

Five
Health Resort

In the first half of the twentieth century a wide range of balneology was still on offer though the popularity of this branch of medical treatment, which was at its height before the First World War, was in decline. This is a fine shot of the exterior of the Thermal or Hot Baths in the 1930s showing the iron and glass colonnading, designed by local architects Bryden & Walton, which was added to the front of the building in 1909. Beneath the canopy can be seen the stone facade of the baths which replaced the original 1854 glass & iron frontage in 1900.

Exterior view of the Natural Baths 1934. The entrance to this bath complex was originally from the side adjoining the Crescent and silvered fountains played in the niches which are now occupied by windows. A major reconstruction of the baths in 1924 made changes to the baths themselves and altered the exterior so that the main entrance was at the front of the building. The Natural Baths building today houses the Tourist Information Centre.

The lobby of the Natural Baths, *c.* 1930. The staircase, going down under the arch on the right of this picture, is the entrance to the baths complex.

The town had its own particular treatment, the Buxton Douche Massage. The patient lay in a shallow bath and was sprayed with water by a bath assistant. There were two versions of the douche, the dry douche was applied to the body without any water in the bath and the wet douche was applied with the body immersed.

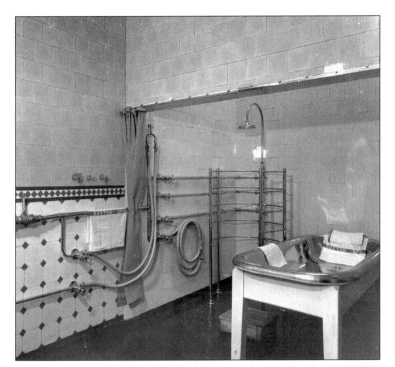

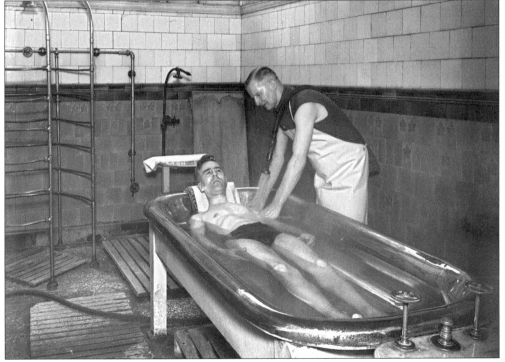

Buxton douche bath in operation. in the 1940s. This shot shows the needle bath on the left. For this the patient stood in the middle of the apparatus and was sprayed with water from all directions through small holes on the inner surfaces of the horizontal pipes. The masseur was Mr Alf Martin who, in later years, became honorary masseur for Stoke City Football Club.

The Ladies Bath at the Natural Baths in 1946. Designed by the Duke of Devonshire's architect, Henry Currey, this bath survives in reasonable condition today.

The same bath being used by a group of men for rehabilitation exercises and remedial games in 1947-8. The bath is not particularly deep, with a shallow sloping floor, which makes it ideal for these purposes.

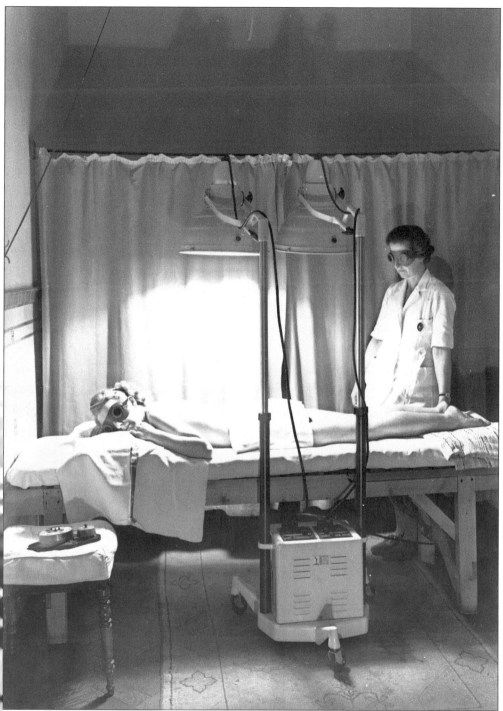

Artificial sunlight treatment was on offer at both the Natural and Hot Baths. As with today's solarium or sun bed the patient was exposed to ultraviolet rays to simulate the effect of sunlight. Sessions were often communal but this photograph shows an individual receiving the treatment in 1948.

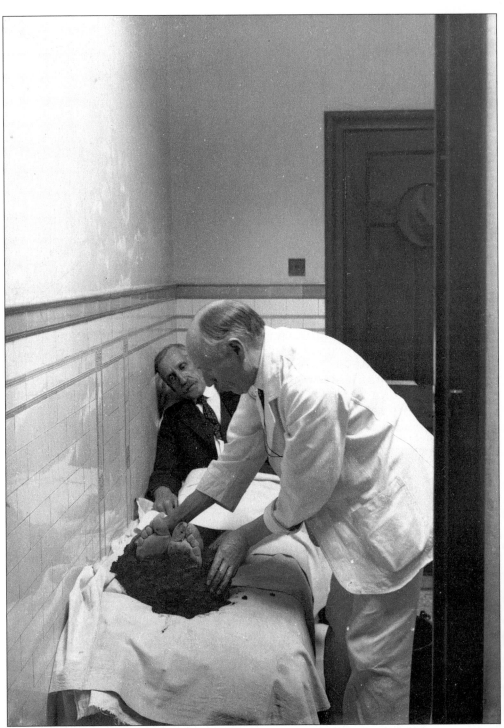

The Buxton Baths offered peat bath treatments in both the Hot and Natural wings. Whole body treatment was the more popular version but, as we see here, treatment with localised applications of peat were also available. It is difficult to discern from the patient's face whether the experience was pleasurable or not!

A Lancashire boiler with two horizontal barrels at the rear of the Hot Baths. Another boiler of the Cornish type with a vertical barrel was also installed. In addition to heating the water in the baths these boilers were used to supply hot water for the for the preparation of moor baths and to the laundry which served both the Hot and Natural Baths. The baths used large quantities of linen in the form of towels, peat sheets and staff uniforms. After the closure of the Charity Hot Baths in George street in 1914 the old baths building was used as public wash baths and the water for these was taken from the Hot Baths boilers. The Hot Baths were closed to the public on 30th September 1963.

The ladies lounge at the Hot Baths in 1928.

The water heating plant at the Hot Baths.

A patient receiving treatment in a small plunge pool at the Natural Baths in 1948.

A patient receiving treatment in a small plunge pool at the Natural Baths in 1948. The crane at the far end of the pool was used to lower the less ambulant patients into the pool, probably using the wheelchair seen in the previous picture.

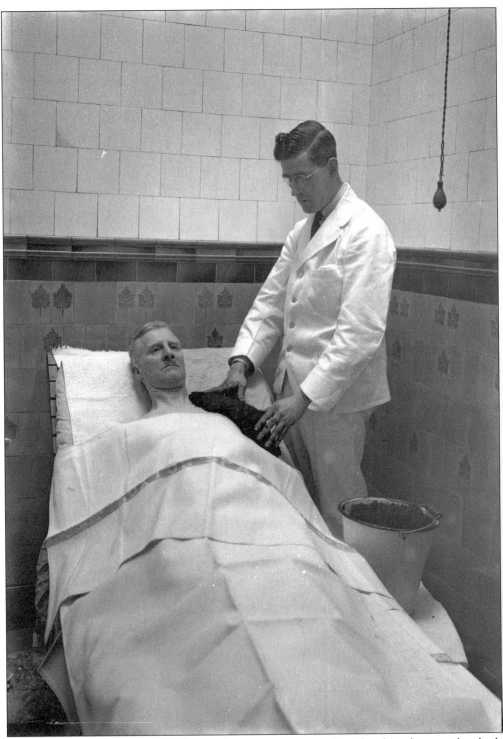

Mr Alf Martin, masseur and bath attendant, poses as a patient for this photograph which demonstrates a shoulder treatment at the Natural Baths.

94

The Gentlemens' first class bath in the Natural Baths, looking east, and showing the semicircular windows which are just a little above road level on the outside. This bath is situated over the main mineral water spring and water entered the bath under its own pressure through holes in the floor slabs of the bath. In later years this was used as the town's main public swimming pool. During excavations below this bath in 1975 a large hoard of Roman coins were found which confirmed that the Romans used Buxton as bathing centre for the whole length of their occupation of Britain. The bath is, today, smaller in size and entirely covered by a perspex dome providing sterile conditions for the water which is taken for bottling.

The lounge, or cooling room, at the Natural Baths as it appeared when photographed for the1946 Buxton Guide. This room is currently occupied by the Tourist Information Centre and can therefore still be viewed by the public.

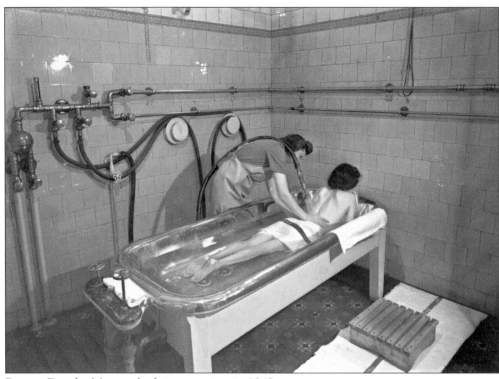

Buxton Douche Massage bath in operation in 1948.

Hot Baths exterior, c. 1964. The cast iron pillars supporting the glass canopy deteriorated seriously from within and the structure was assessed as unsafe and removed in the early 1970s. This revealed the facade of 1900 which can still be seen today.

Devonshire Hospital from the Quadrant. Originally built as stables and riding ring for the Duke of Devonshire 1784/9, it was converted to half stables and half hospital in 1859 and then completely to a hospital in 1881 when the giant dome was erected over the formerly exposed central circle of the building. The conversion was designed by local architect, Robert Rippon Duke and at the time was one of the largest unsupported domes in the world. Its diameter is 138 ft, larger than St Paul's in London (112ft), similar to St Peter's in Rome (138ft) and only just smaller than the Duomo in Florence (139ft). The hospital acquired its 'Royal' title in 1934 from King George V in recognition of the work done by the Buxton Bath Charity. In 1948 the Devonshire Royal Hospital was absorbed into the National Health Service.

The interior of the dome at the Devonshire Hospital. The square area in the middle of the floor was the site of a plaster statue of the 7th Duke of Devonshire. The area under the dome has been used for games and remedial training. A most remarkable echo can be experienced when standing in the centre of the dome and a 'whispering gallery' effect exists at the perimeter.

An Austin ambulance with patients and staff outside the Devonshire Hospital in 1935.

The Devonshire Hospital gymnasium in 1935.

A group of staff at the Devonshire Royal Hospital outside the main entrance after an award ceremony in 1965. Back row, from left to right: Marion Hambleton, -?-, Dorothy Bentley, Elizabeth Syrincki, Mrs M. Lee. Front row: Matron Blake-Mahon, an official of the Health service, Jean Webster (nurse tutor).

Devonshire Hospital main canteen and theatre as it appeared in the mid-1930s.

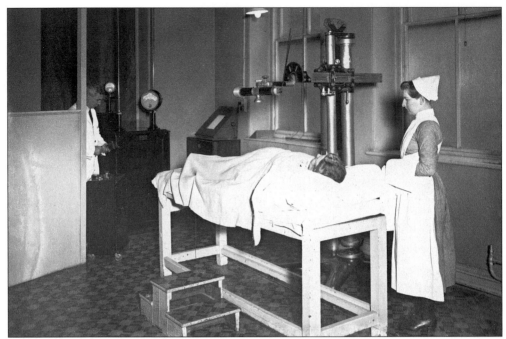

Devonshire Hospital X-Ray department with equipment which by today's standards seems rather basic. The x-ray tube is of the stationary anode type and appears to have very little in-built radiation protection. The equipment was a Victor Wantz junior x-ray set with a rotary disc rectifier and was installed in 1929. The high tension cables seen rising from the generator at the back of the picture are not heavily insulated, even though during an x-ray exposure they would have a potential difference of about 80 kilovolts. In seventy years we have seen remarkable advances in x-ray technology.

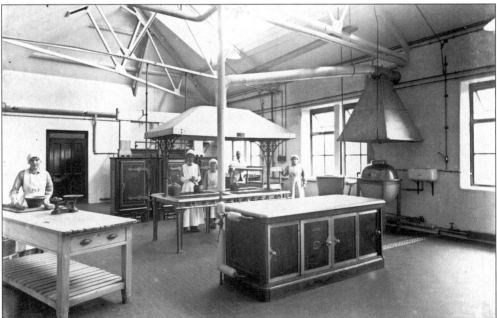

The Devonshire Hospital kitchen in the 1930s.

HRH Princess Mary at the laying of the foundation stone of the new wing at the Devonshire Hospital. On her left is the Ninth Duke of Devonshire. The wing provided a ground floor dining room with a staff dining room and kitchens on the first floor. The inscription reads 'This stone was laid by HRH Princess Mary on 29th October 1921 in commemoration of the services rendered by the Devonshire Hospital during the Great War 1914-1918.'

Exterior of the new wing shortly after its completion. It was built by the local firm of H. Robinson who also built St Mary's church in Dale Road.

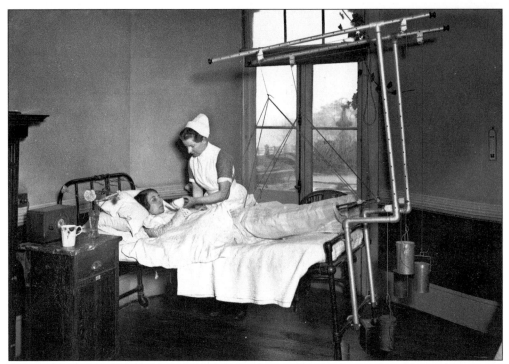

A young patient in leg traction on an orthopaedic ward at the Devonshire Hospital in around 1938.

Critchlow's private invalid car photographed at the West End Garage in August 1932. This is an interesting reminder of pre-NHS ambulance days. Critchlows advertised their services, among other places, at the local cinema.

Cavendish Girls School, south aspect. The plans for this building were drawn up by the Duke of Devonshire's architect, Henry Currey in 1856. It was intended to build this as a hospital, in Sylvan Park, for patients of the Buxton Bath Charity. The site was not thought to be suitable, however, and eventually the duke allowed part of the Great Stables building to be converted to accommodate the charity patients. The plans were used in 1861 to build Wye House, an asylum for the care and treatment of the insane of the 'higher and middle classes'.

Cavendish Girls School, south aspect. Wye House ceased to be used as a lunatic asylum in 1901 and the inmates were moved over the road to Corbar Hill House which was renamed Wye House. In September 1912 the Ninth Duke of Devonshire donated the original Wye House premises to the school authorities creating the Cavendish Girls School. It achieved grammar school status in 1945. Girls educated there would have noticed remaining evidence of its use as an asylum. Some rooms had bars on the windows and others appeared to have been used as padded cells. From 1991 the new Community School in College Road consolidated all secondary education on one site and the Cavendish provision, by then Buxton Girls Upper School, was gradually closed. The building was demolished in 1993.

Buxton Hospital was built in 1912 to the designs of local architects Bryden & Walton. The second annual report of the Buxton District Cottage Hospital was happy to report that the finances of the establishment were in a healthy condition and that the cost of running the hospital for the previous year was £633 4s 7d! Over the years much expansion has taken place beginning with the addition of ten childrens cots in 1920. A further extension, costing £7,767, was opened on 26 April 1924 by the Duke of Devonshire. An x-ray room was incorporated into the hospital on Sunday 8 March 1925 by Dr Higgins, radiologist of Manchester and Miss E.W. Pilkington was appointed as its first radiographer. Interestingly the x-ray equipment, costing £523, was purchased by Herbert Frood who founded the local brake lining firm, Ferodo. A lodge to house the resident caretaker (known today as The Bungalow) was built in the grounds of the hospital in 1929.

Buxton Hospital Childrens Ward Extension. A public appeal was launched in the town to raise £6000 for the construction of a childrens ward at the cottage hospital. Although less than half this sum was raised by 1929 the extension was added to the hospital in that year. The building was designed by local architect, Charles Flint. This unit was originally linked to the main hospital by a glazed corridor with an open walkway along its roof. This was later enclosed by a glazed walkway (today referred to as The Bridge) and the the lower floor glazing has been replaced by solid walls. The whole of the middle foreground of this photograph is now occupied by clinic areas and the hospital's main waiting room.

Buxton Hospital children's ward extension seen from Sherbrook in 1929. The land which slopes away from this extension has now been levelled to provide car parking.

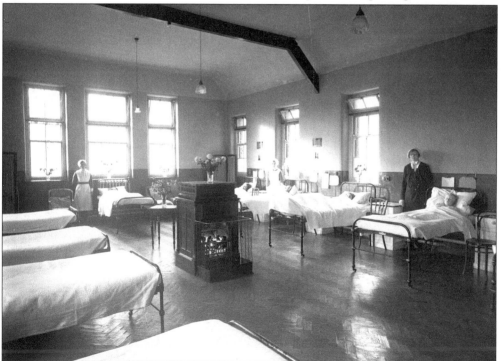

Interior view of the childrens ward at Buxton Hospital in about 1930, showing the solid fuel heating system situated in the middle of the ward.

Buxton is a hill town with business areas on two main levels. Higher Buxton provides the market place and streets leading off it for shopping. The Lower town offers Spring Gardens and the Quadrant, together with the Crescent, Baths and areas of commerce around them. The principle connection is Terrace Road. Here is Skidmore's shop at the top of Terrace Road photographed in March 1946 with the outside stairs still in use. This building was originally stables for the adjacent Buxton House. The bull's-eye windows on the side of this building still survive today.

Six
Higher and Lower Town

Delivery of beer to the New Inn in the early 1930s. In the days of real ale it was heavy work handling the large barrels. The landlord stands in the doorway supervising the draymen.

Two views of the same buildings separated by four years. This view shows the premises of Liddel's the chemist in 1928. An attractive corner property which looks vacant.

By July 1932 the property had been acquired by the Halifax Building Society and remodelled. The building society had, in fact, moved from next door as the previous photograph shows. Apart from the removal of one set of bay windows, the frontage looks much the same today.

A view of the Market Place in about 1930 showing the Town Hall. The Market Cross in the centre was moved in 1949 to its present position in front of the KwiK Save shop alongside the public pump.

The council chamber in the Town Hall in the 1930s.

The Eagle Hotel in May 1934 and part of the Eagle Parade. On the left are the Corporation Gas showrooms.

The Market Place in about 1930 showing the Town Hall, built by local builder James Salt, and opened in 1889. At this time it still had its open colonnades. A variety of heavy saloon cars are parked here, note the solid tyres on the lorry. This photograph was probably taken for publication as a postcard or for the town guide.

A fine shot of the Eagle Hotel, part of the Eagle Parade and the gas showrooms. The Austin Heavy Twelve model in the foreground dates this photograph to about 1933.

This photograph was taken in the late 1950s and, apart from tree growth and the resiting of the Market Cross, very little has changed. The gas showrooms are still adjacent to the Eagle Hotel. In this earlier age of public transport, however, the bus station occupied the area in front of the Town Hall.

A busy scene looking east wards down Spring Gardens from the base of the Slopes in about 1933. Behind the car is the Royal Hotel which was built in 1851 and replaced an earlier hotel on the same site, the Angel inn. In the eighteenth century Spring Gardens was known as Sheffield Road.

The base of the Slopes from the Hot Baths in the early 1930s. Appearing from behind the tree to the left is the spire of the Congregational church on Hardwick Street which was demolished in 1983 and replaced by a block of flats. The 'No Parking' sign on the road prevented car parking on the bathchair stand.

Turners Memorial at the junction of Terrace Road and the Quadrant in 1933. The memorial is seen on this photograph sporting an electric lamp which replaced the original gas lamp in the early 1900s. 'Turner's' was a popular meeting place and the local bus service used it as a terminal. The monument was erected in memory of local townsman, Samuel Turner in 1879 but was damaged by a stray vehicle in the early 1960s and was put in storage. It was restored and re-erected in 1994 complete with a replica of the original gas lamp, manufactured by the same company who made the first lamp, Sugg lighting of Crawley, West Sussex.

A view down Terrace Road in the 1940s showing Turner's Memorial on the left and the Quadrant overlooked by the Palace Hotel.

An RAC officer is apparently directing traffic (or perhaps welcoming people into the Westminster Bank!) in this view at the corner of Spring Gardens and Terrace Road. The bottom shop on Terrace Road just above the Bank is tenanted by the Leek & Moorlands Building Society.

The Hot Baths, Quadrant and west end of Spring Gardens seen from Terrace Road in 1938. The local bus is seen waiting to take on passengers at 'Turner's'. The tree behind the bus in the picture was a well known feature and will be remembered by many Buxtonians. The 'Spa of Blue Waters' was a Buxton slogan adopted in the 1930s.

Another view of Turner's memorial in about 1954 from under the arcade of the Hot Baths. On the left of this view is the Grove Hotel which dates back to early 1770 when it was called the Grove Coffee House. It was used as a boarding stop for the Manchester, Derby and London coaches in the early 1800s and shops were added to the ground floor at the end of the nineteenth century.

Spring Gardens from the Slopes in about 1965. The banner across the road advertises a county cricket match.

No book on Buxton would be complete without some coverage of the weather, especially cold, snowy weather! Both J.R. Board and J.D. Meddins took advantage of some of the more spectacular winters to record how the town looked and coped. Often, after the blizzards have immobilised the town, the sun comes out and provides photographers with the right conditions to capture the handywork of a storm. Few of the mechanical aids relied on today are in evidence in these old photographs - except perhaps the odd quarry bulldozer - but the main snow clearing machine was man and shovel as it had always been. Looking back it seems amazing that, after some of the massive snow falls endured, the town got back on the move just as quickly as it does now. Today's snow falls never seem quite as big as big as these old ones! The picture above sums up the bus traveller's lot during these times. A Buxton bound bus is abandoned at Waterswallows leaving the passengers with a cold, but no doubt pleasant, walk into town through Fairfield.

Seven

Buxton Weather

The hardy bulldozer driver (no cab for him!) slowly clears a way round the abandoned bus and other vehicles to allow the passage of other road users.

One must admire our hardy photographer, in this case, John Meddins, who would have spent hours plodding over Fairfield Common to get these unique shots between the Peak Forest turning and Bibbington's. They portray the mammoth task ahead of the snow clearing teams. When snow fell in this quantity, one of the greatest problems, in addition to how to move it, was where to move it to. The picture above shows the principle of 'stepping' used by the railways to assist the passage of a mechanical plough, but there is a long way to go before the road can be opened. Note also the 'finger' type signpost suffering from considerable wind movement and pointing in the wrong direction! The pictures on these pages were taken in the great 1947 snow.

A vivid illustration of how snow clearing was done by hand. During the war German and Italian prisoners of war were used a great deal in the Peak District for snow clearing, both on road and rail.

This photograph demonstrates not only the size of the task that sometimes faces the road clearers after a big snowfall but also just how beautiful the snow drifts can look.

These two pictures show relief arriving for a cluster of abandoned North-Western buses at the Peak Forest turning. Having got through, the next job was to move the frozen vehicles prior to a proper snow clearance.

Finally the bulldozer's efforts show results and limited traffic movement is possible on the Waterswallow's Road.

Two views a little closer to the town show the hardy snow clearers, well 'bagged-up' against the weather, employing the traditional method of snow riddance.

Two views of the Devonshire Royal Hospital under snow conditions. The upper picture dates from the 1930s whilst the lower one is from the 1940s.

This view, from the early 1960s, shows a boy posting a letter in the Victorian hexagonal 'Penfold' post box opposite the Opera House.

This early morning shot shows the centre of town devoid of any vehicles and people after a light fall of snow during the night.

The weight of snow lowers the branches of trees adjacent to the Union Club above, whilst, below, St John's church looks very picturesque with its snow covered surrounding trees.

This is a wonderful photograph of a five horse-powered street plough in action in Dale Road in the 1920s. It is hard to believe that a similar plough was involved in a fatal accident in 1933. After a sudden and very heavy fall of snow, on 22 and 23 February, the plough was being operated by a team of three men in Ashwood Dale. One of the team, Mr John Marsden, was walking alongside the horses when he slipped, fell and was run over by the plough.

The same snow that brings chaos and hard work for the older generation provides lots of fun for the young. The town boasted some good sledging facilities, and still does. Here two boys head up College Road towards a well known run on Temple Fields (see p. 73).

Despite the conditions work must go on. Here the driver of a Post Office telephone van prepares his vehicle for action at the garage yard in Palace Road in the late 1940s.

The Cheshire Cheese public house on High Street under snow and, judging by the grey sky, there was more to come!

Carol singers enjoy a really seasonal setting as they sing outside the Spa Hotel. J.R. Board exhibited a similar photograph to this at the International Exhibition of Professional Photography in 1925.

Acknowledgements

We want to thank those who have helped with this publication. Firstly Derbyshire County Council, Libraries and Museum Service who have given permission for us to reproduce the images in this book. All the photographs except those on pp 4 and 6, have been taken from the Board Collection held at the Buxton Museum and Art Gallery. We are grateful to the curator and staff of the museum for their help, also the staff at the Buxton library, local studies department for providing such an excellent service. Mrs Barbara Ingham (nee Meddins) very kindly agreed to see us, gave us a good lunch and provided background information and photographs on the Board and Meddins families. A number of people have helped us with captioning and other information, they are: Graeme Marshall, Henry Sherwood, Peter Monks, Maureen Howe, Rita Urion and Jean Lee. Special thanks go to Chris Bentley for his photographic expertise. Finally we thank our 'local historian emeritus', Oliver Gomersal, for carrying out a final edit on the book in his usual meticulous manner.

JMB, MJL, CW
Buxton
Summer 1999